THE WHITE HOUSE

Jessica Morrison
and Heather Kissock

www.av2books.com

AV² provides enriched content that supplements and complements this book. Weigl's AV² books strive to create inspired learning and engage young minds in a total learning experience.

Your AV² Media Enhanced books come alive with...

 Audio
Listen to sections of the book read aloud.

 Key Words
Study vocabulary, and complete a matching word activity.

 Video
Watch informative video clips.

 Quizzes
Test your knowledge.

 **Embedded Weblinks**
Gain additional information for research.

Slide Show
View images and captions, and prepare a presentation.

Go to **www.av2books.com**, and enter this book's unique code.

BOOK CODE

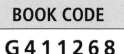

G 4 1 1 2 6 8

AV² **by Weigl** brings you media enhanced books that support active learning.

Try This!
Complete activities and hands-on experiments.

...and much, much more!

Published by AV² by Weigl
350 5th Avenue, 59th Floor
New York, NY 10118

Website: www.av2books.com   www.weigl.com

Library of Congress Cataloging-in-Publication Data
Morrison, Jessica.
 The White House / Jessica Morrison and Heather Kissock.
   p. cm. -- (Virtual field trip)
 Includes index.
 ISBN 978-1-61913-253-5 (hardcover : alk. paper) -- ISBN 978-1-61913-259-7 (softcover : alk. paper)
 1. White House (Washington, D.C.)--Juvenile literature. 2. Washington (D.C.)--Buildings, structures, etc.--Juvenile literature. I. Kissock, Heather. II. Title.
 F204.W5M67 2012
 975.3--dc23
                    2011045451

Printed in the United States of America in North Mankato, Minnesota
1 2 3 4 5 6 7 8 9 0 16 15 14 13 12

012012
WEP060112

Editor: Heather Kissock
Design: Terry Paulhus

Every reasonable effort has been made to trace ownership and to obtain permission to reprint copyright material. The publishers would be pleased to have any errors or omissions brought to their attention so that they may be corrected in subsequent printings.

Weigl acknowledges Getty Images as its primary image supplier for this title.

Contents

What is the White House?

For centuries, kings, queens, and other world leaders have lived in grand homes, such as castles, palaces, and mansions. As the home of the president of the United States, the White House is one such place. Located in Washington, D.C., the White House is one of the best-known structures in the world. It stands as a symbol of power and excellence.

The White House was built following the American Revolutionary War, a conflict between the American **colonies** and England, their mother country. In 1776, the men who were leading the war wrote a letter to the king of England. This letter was called the Declaration of Independence. It announced to England and the world that the United States was no longer a British colony. The colonies had united to become an independent country, with its own laws and leaders.

The young country struggled to organize itself. In 1790, the government decided to build a city that would serve as its permanent national capital. This city was going to be called Washington, after the country's first president, George Washington. The city was to be the center of activity for the country's government and its citizens. The White House was the first building to be built in the new city.

The White House was built solely to serve as the residence of the president of the United States.

Snapshot of the District of Columbia

The District of Columbia is located in the northeast United States. It covers an area of 68 square miles (176 square kilometers) and sits on the Virginia–Maryland border.

INTRODUCING D.C.

CAPITAL CITY: Washington

FLAG:

MOTTO: *Justia Omnibus* (Justice for All)

NICKNAME: The Nation's Capital

POPULATION: 601,723 (2010)

FOUNDED: July 16, 1790

CLIMATE: Subtropical, with four distinct seasons

SUMMER TEMPERATURE: Average of 79° Fahrenheit (26° Celsius)

WINTER TEMPERATURE: Average of 38°F (3°C)

TIME ZONE: Eastern Standard Time (EST)

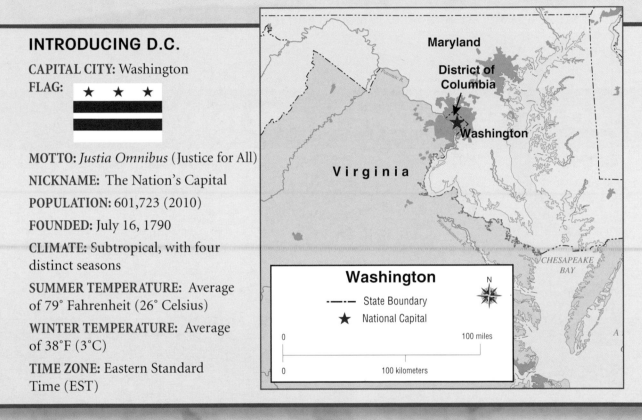

Maryland

District of Columbia

Washington

Virginia

CHESAPEAKE BAY

Washington

N

-·-·- State Boundary

★ National Capital

0   100 miles

0   100 kilometers

District of Columbia Symbols

The District of Columbia has several official symbols. Some symbols represent the features that distinguish the area from other parts of the United States. Others indicate the unique place D.C. has in the history of the country.

OFFICIAL FLOWER
American Beauty Rose

OFFICIAL BIRD
Wood Thrush

OFFICIAL TREE
Scarlet Oak

A Step Back in Time

When George Washington decided to build a place for future presidents to live, he held a contest to create the best design for "The President's House." The winner of this contest would become the building's **architect** and win $500. An Irish immigrant, James Hoban, was chosen for his design.

Construction of the White House started in 1792. By 1797, the walls stood, and the roof was almost complete. Windows and interior walls were installed over the next three years.

CONSTRUCTION TIMELINE

AD 1792
The **cornerstone** of the White House is laid by George Washington.

1801–1809
Thomas Jefferson, the country's third president, has two **colonnades** built on each side of the White House.

1814
The White House is set on fire by the British Army during the **War of 1812**. It is rebuilt and opens again three years later.

1830–1880
Running water, heating systems, and the building's first telephone are installed.

When originally designed, the White House was to be four times the size of the one that was actually built.

The British set fire to the White House after the American forces set fire to the city of York, or present-day Toronto, in what is now Canada.

Although much of the White House's construction was overseen by George Washington, he never lived in it. John Adams was the first president to live in the White House. He moved into the house in 1800, when it was almost finished. When Adams and his wife arrived, many of the walls still had wet plaster.

In 1790, Congress enacted the Residence Act, giving President Washington the authority to choose a location for the White House.

1890–1900
Electric lighting is added, along with air conditioning and a large main kitchen.

1902
The West **Wing** is built.

1942
The East Wing is built.

1940–1950
Security is improved when the U.S. joins World War II. Special outdoor lighting is installed.

1979
The first solar panels are installed to help with energy conservation.

The West Wing was built during Theodore Roosevelt's presidency. It was part of a major White House renovation commissioned by the president.

The White House Location

When George Washington chose the site of the White House, he decided on land that was only 16 miles (26 km) north of his home in Mount Vernon, Virginia. Today, the White House is located at 1600 Pennsylvania Avenue, in Washington, D.C. It is situated on a hill overlooking the Potomac River.

The grounds around the White House are called President's Park. The White House and its grounds cover 18 acres (7.3 hectares).

Pennsylvania Avenue connects the White House to the U.S. Capitol.

The White House Today

Today, the White House is the oldest building in Washington, D.C. It is also the only private residence of a head of state that is open to the public free of charge. Every day, more than 6,000 people visit the White House to tour the grounds and the building itself.

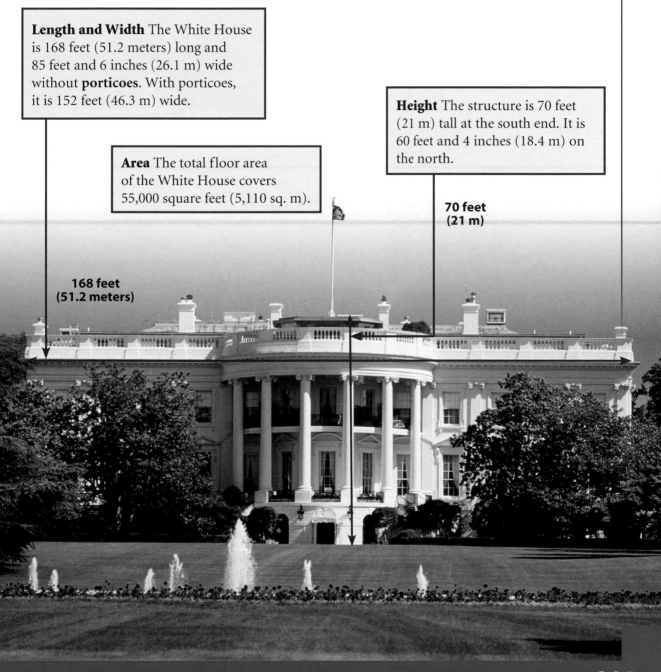

Length and Width The White House is 168 feet (51.2 meters) long and 85 feet and 6 inches (26.1 m) wide without **porticoes**. With porticoes, it is 152 feet (46.3 m) wide.

Height The structure is 70 feet (21 m) tall at the south end. It is 60 feet and 4 inches (18.4 m) on the north.

Area The total floor area of the White House covers 55,000 square feet (5,110 sq. m).

70 feet
(21 m)

168 feet
(51.2 meters)

Outside the White House

*The White House is a building with a **neoclassical** style. Most neoclassical buildings are symmetrical. This means they look the same on both left and right sides. Neoclassical buildings also have tall columns at the front and triangular **pediments** on the roof.*

Symmetry The White House was built in such a way that each side is in balance with the other. In other words, both the left and right sides of the building share the same features in exactly the same place. Windows, columns, and doorways are placed in the exact position on each side of the building. As a result of this placement, the center of the building becomes the **focal point**.

The White House is an example of Palladian architecture. Based on the work of Italian architect, Andrea Palladio, buildings in this style are known for their use of symmetry.

The open colonnade links the residence part of the White House to the West Wing. The president walks this route to reach his office.

Colonnades The White House features two large colonnades that connect the main building with its two wings. Only one of the colonnades is enclosed with glass panels. The other one remains open, meaning that people walking through it are exposed to the open air.

The north portico was added to the White House sometime around 1830.

North Portico The White House has two porticoes. The north portico is square in shape and serves as the main entrance to the White House. It is here that the president greets official guests. The north portico has a triangular pediment and is supported by Ionic columns. Columns in the Ionic style are slender and topped by **volutes**.

It is believed that the windows at the White House are bullet-proof.

Windows The White House has 147 windows. On the outside of the building, most of these windows are capped with pediments. The first floor pediments are either triangular or rounded in shape. On the second floor, they are flat.

South Portico The south portico is rounded and opens onto the south lawn. A staircase sits on each side. The south portico also features Ionic columns but lacks a pediment due to its shape. This portico does, however, have a balcony. It was added by President Harry S. Truman in 1948. The south portico is used during ceremonies and informal gatherings that often take place on the south lawn.

The south portico was built in 1824. The president at the time was James Monroe.

VIRTUAL TOUR

Visitors to the White House have to request a visit through their Member of Congress. International visitors must submit a request through their **embassy**.

Inside the White House

The White House has three main parts. The residence is the central building. This is where the president and his family live. The West Wing contains the offices of the president and other staff. The East Wing has offices for the First Lady and her staff.

Entrance Hall The entrance hall sits inside the north portico. This is where most foreign officials are greeted when they visit the White House. The entrance hall is a large, square room, measuring about 31 by 44 feet (9.5 by 13.4 m). Its floors are made of pink marble. The east wall of the entrance hall opens to the grand staircase. The president escorts his guests down the staircase for receptions and other events.

Journalists sometimes attend press conferences in the Entrance Hall.

The Red Room maintains its color theme throughout the year. Even Christmas decorations are primarily red.

Reception Rooms
Throughout the year, numerous events take place in the White House. The White House has four rooms designed to receive incoming guests. The East Room is the largest room in the White House. Large functions, such as concerts and press conferences, are often held here. The Blue Room, the Green Room, and the Red Room are named for their colorful decor. Besides being used to receive guests, these smaller rooms are sometimes used for dinner parties.

Oval Office The Oval Office is located in the West Wing and serves as the president's office. It is here that the president has private meetings with visiting officials and his staff. The room is named for its shape. The focal point of the Oval Office is the president's desk. It is from here that the president addresses the nation during television broadcasts.

Each president has the right to add his or her own personal touches to the room. This includes changing drapery, furniture, and carpets.

Lincoln Bedroom The Lincoln Bedroom is on the second floor of the White House. The room is named for President Abraham Lincoln, who used it as an office. It became a bedroom later and is now used as a guest room for distinguished visitors. The room includes the huge 8 foot by 6 foot (2.4 by 1.8 m) Lincoln bed.

The Lincoln Bedroom has its own sitting room, where guests can relax and have private time.

State Dining Room When foreign heads of state visit the White House, a large, formal dinner is usually held. The State Dining Room can seat up to 140 guests. Seating arrangements can vary, but the guests of honor are usually seated at the long mahogany dining table.

Under President Jefferson, the State Dining Room became an office and library. When President Jackson came to office, it was reverted back to a dining room.

Big Ideas Behind the White House

Building a house for the president was no easy task. It required careful design, planning, and hard work. To make sure that the White House would stay strong and sturdy, workers had to use their knowledge of science.

Before it was whitewashed, the White House was gray. This is the natural color of Virginia sandstone.

Properties of Sandstone

The government chose sandstone to construct the exterior of the White House. Sandstone is easy to shape and carve, but it is not a very hard stone. Rain, ice, and snow can leak into it, making it crumble and crack over time. A white liquid called whitewash was applied to the stone to keep it strong. Whitewash is made of water and a substance called **quicklime**. When it is painted on stone, it looks milky and white. When carbon dioxide in the air hits it, a process called carbonatation occurs. The calcium in the whitewash combines with the carbon in the air and changes into a hard, chalky material called calcium carbonate. This material provides a hard coating for the sandstone, helping it resist the effects of **weathering**.

Loads

When building any structure, planners have to take **loads** into consideration. The building must be made to support its own weight and the weight of its contents, as well as resist the forces that affect it, such as wind and **gravity**. The White House uses columns as a way of supporting the building's load. Columns help the structure resist the pull of gravity. When a structure is heavy, its weight pushes down. Columns help to spread the downward force across a bigger area. By spreading the weight out, the building is less likely to fall.

Columns come in many shapes and sizes. To support a heavy weight, builders can use a few thick columns or many thin ones.

Science at Work at the White House

People did not have power tools to help them build the White House. Instead, they used simple machines to help ease their workload. Simple machines help make a hard job easier by using scientific principles.

To get to the White House, the sandstone was loaded on to wooden wagons. It was then taken to the Potomac River, where it was loaded on a boat and shipped to Washington.

Wheels and Axles

White House construction workers did not have trucks to transport the heavy sandstone. Instead, wagons were filled with stones and then taken where they needed to be. Wagons use wheels and axles to move across the ground. The wheel and axle is a two-part simple machine. Wheels rotate, so they reduce the **friction** between the moving object and the ground. The axle is the structure that attaches the wheel to the rest of the wagon. By using wagons with wheels and axles, builders could move large loads of sandstone. Even wagons full of stones and people would move easily along the ground because of the reduced friction.

Pulleys

The sandstone used to build the White House came from a **quarry** in Virginia. Getting the sandstone out of the quarry was a difficult job. The stones had to be lifted very high, against the pull of gravity. To lift the heavy stones, workers used pulleys. A pulley is a wheel with a groove around the edge. A rope sits inside the groove. Pulling on one side of the rope causes the wheel to turn. This moves the other end of the rope in the opposite direction. Pulleys make lifting easier because they work with gravity. Instead of pulling stones up to the top of the quarry, workers pulled down on the pulley rope to lift stones up. Pulling down is much easier than pulling up, so workers could complete the job more easily.

A pulley uses a wheel to distribute the weight of the object being lifted. This makes the object feel lighter.

VIRTUAL TOUR

The White House exterior is still made of its original sandstone.

The White House Builders

It took more than eight years to build the original White House, and many improvements have been made over the years. However, building a house is about more than the structure. What goes inside and around it is also important. Many people worked hard to make the White House and its surroundings fit for a president.

James Hoban Architect

When George Washington announced the contest to find an architect, nine people entered their designs. Washington hired James Hoban to build the White House, after seeing his vision for the building.

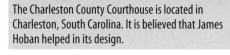

James Hoban was an Irish architect who built many American buildings. He was born in Kilkenny County, Ireland, in 1762. Hoban studied architecture at the Royal Dublin Society before sailing to America. By 1785, he had arrived in Philadelphia and established himself as an architect. Two years later,

The Charleston County Courthouse is located in Charleston, South Carolina. It is believed that James Hoban helped in its design.

he moved to South Carolina, where he built many public buildings. He soon became well known for his talent as an architect and builder. In 1791, while Hoban was still in South Carolina, George Washington became aware of Hoban's work and encouraged him to enter the design competition for the White House. Hoban was chosen as the winner one year later.

The Capitol serves as the center of government for the United States Congress. James Hoban supervised part of its construction.

James Hoban did such a good job on the White House that he was hired again to rebuild it after the fire in 1814. He later designed the porticoes on the north and south ends of the building. These were added in 1824 and 1829. His relationship with the government continued when he was hired as one of the supervising architects on the construction of the Capitol.

Sculptors

Sculptors often use tools called chisels to shape stone.

Sculptors carve pictures and designs out of stone or other substances. All of the sculptures on the White House doors, walls, and pediments were carved by stone sculptors. They used tools such as knives to shape the stone, and polished their finished work to smooth out the edges. The sculptors used a tube that looked like a drinking straw to blow away bits of stone as they sculpted. Today, sculptors use many of the same tools in their work. As sculpting is such careful work, it can take a long time to produce one piece of art.

Interior Decorators

Interior designers plan how a room should look. In the White House, interior designers used color, lighting, furniture, and paintings to make each room look special. This kind of work requires much imagination and creativity. It is important for the designers to make rooms beautiful, but also useful. The first White House interior designers planned with pencils and paper. Today, computers are used to sketch out designs and plans.

Besides creating attractive interiors, interior designers also have to consider the safety and well-being of the people who will use the space.

Landscape Gardeners

Landscape gardeners often need to use local plants in their designs, so they must know a great deal about botany. This is the scientific study of plant life.

Landscape gardeners designed and developed the White House gardens. They used flowers, trees, rocks, and fountains to make the gardens look beautiful. Landscape gardeners do all sorts of jobs. They plant trees and flowers, build rock gardens, and mow grass lawns. They even create fountains and ponds for people to enjoy. There is some heavy lifting and a great deal of moving, so landscape gardeners need to be in good shape to do most jobs.

Similar Structures Around the World

Neoclassical structures like the White House are found all over the world. They are built from different types of stone and wood. Many are protected by governments to keep them preserved.

Leinster House

BUILT: 1745–1747
LOCATION: Dublin, Ireland
DESIGN: Richard Cassels
DESCRIPTION: Leinster House is a three-story building built of stone. It was named after the Duke of Leinster, who bought the house in 1815. When the White House was being designed, James Hoban used Leinster House as his model. Today, the building is home to the National Parliament of Ireland.

The Romanian Athenaeum was built using money collected from a fund-raising campaign.

Leinster House was originally known as Kildare House. It was named after the Earl of Kildare, the man who ordered its construction. It was renamed Leinster House when the earl became the Duke of Leinster.

Romanian Athenaeum

BUILT: 1888–1897
LOCATION: Bucharest, Romania
DESIGN: Albert Galleron
DESCRIPTION: The Romanian Athenaeum is a concert hall built in the neoclassical style. In 2007, the concert hall was added to the list of the Label of European Heritage Sites. This is a program that identifies culturally important buildings in the European Union.

United States Supreme Court Building

BUILT: 1932–1935
LOCATION: Washington, D.C.
DESIGN: Cass Gilbert
DESCRIPTION: The United States Supreme Court Building is a four-story structure made of marble and white oak. The west entrance features 16 columns that hold up marble containing the motto, "Equal Justice Under Law." The east entrance features the motto "Justice the Guardian of Liberty."

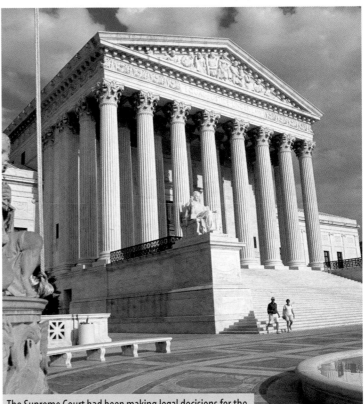

The Supreme Court had been making legal decisions for the country for 145 years before it was given its own building.

Monticello

Monticello is the only house in the United States to be listed as a United Nations World Heritage Site.

BUILT: 1769–1784, with additional construction from 1796–1809
LOCATION: Charlottesville, Virginia
DESIGN: Thomas Jefferson
DESCRIPTION: Monticello was the home of Thomas Jefferson, the United States' third president. Like many neoclassical buildings, the house features a dome, columns, and porticoes. In 1987, Monticello was designated a **World Heritage Site**, ensuring its preservation for years to come.

Issues Facing the White House

Structures can impact the environment. Energy created from **fossil fuels** and the space the building takes up all have an impact on the land. In recent years, various presidents and their governments have taken steps to ensure that the White House does not have a negative effect on the environment.

WHAT WAS THE ISSUE?

Non-renewable energy sources, such as coal and oil, were used to power the White House.

Heating and air conditioning systems were outdated.

EFFECTS

Once non-renewable energy sources are used, they are gone forever. Limiting their use and finding renewable energy sources will ensure power in the future.

Outdated equipment resulted in inefficient energy use. The machinery was using more electricity than necessary to operate.

ACTION TAKEN

In 2003, the government installed solar panels at the White House to supply electricity to the grounds and to heat the water. Solar power is a renewable resource.

In 1994, the heating and air conditioning systems at the White House were upgraded.

Build Cup Columns

Columns support the weight of many structures around the world. Architects have two options when using columns to hold up heavy materials. They can use a few thick, heavy columns, or they can use several thin, lightweight columns.

Experiment with these two options by making your own building. Use paper cups as columns and cardboard as the roof. You can use your own weight to test the strength of your columns.

Materials
- small paper drinking cups
- 2 thick cardboard squares, 20 inches by 20 inches (51 cm by 51 cm) each
- sand
- a pencil
- a towel or sheet (optional)

Instructions

1. Try this activity outside, or on a towel or sheet.

2. Place the cups face down on the first cardboard square, in any design you like. Use as many as you think you will need.

3. Place the second cardboard square on top of the cups.

4. Carefully step onto the cardboard sheet, using a wall or friend to spot you. Do the columns support your weight? If they did, try using fewer cups to see how many you need. If they did not, add more cups until your weight is supported.

5. Once you know how many cups will support you, remove one or two.

6. Fill the remaining cups with sand. To do this, place them face down on the cardboard, and pierce small holes in them with a pencil. Then, pour the sand through the holes.

7. Now, try standing on them. Do they support your weight?

8. Experiment with different numbers of cups. Fill some with sand, and leave some empty. Do different arrangements support your weight better?

White House Quiz

Q Who was the original architect for the White House?

A James Hoban

Q How was the White House architect determined?

A James Hoban became the White House architect after winning a design competition.

Q What are the characteristics of neoclassical architecture?

A Columns, symmetry, and triangular pediments on the roof

Q How do columns help support a building?

A Columns help support buildings by distributing the weight across a larger surface.

Words to Know

architect: a person who designs and supervises the construction of buildings

colonies: settlements owned by another country

colonnades: a series of columns at regular intervals, supporting a roof

cornerstone: a stone placed at the corner of a building during a ceremony to mark the start of construction

embassy: a building that houses the representatives of a foreign country

focal point: the central point of attention

fossil fuels: fuels that are made from plant or animal remains; for example, coal, natural gas, and petroleum

friction: a force that slows down motion when surfaces slide against each other

gravity: the force that moves objects toward the center of Earth

loads: weights or sources of pressure carried by objects

neoclassical: a style of building that is taken from ancient Greece and Rome; normally uses columns, symmetry, and triangular pediments on the roof

non-renewable: a resource that cannot be replaced through natural processes

pediments: structures that are usually placed on top of columns

porticoes: covered porches

quarry: a place where rock is extracted from the ground

quicklime: substance created by heating limestone, also called calcium oxide

volutes: spiral, scroll-like ornaments

War of 1812: a war between Great Britain and the United States, fought chiefly along the Canadian border from 1812 to 1814

weathering: the breaking down of rocks and other materials by the action of wind, rain, and other elements

wing: a structure attached to and connected internally with the side of a building

World Heritage Site: a site designated by the United Nations to be of great cultural worth to the world and in need of protection

Index

Log on to www.av2books.com

AV² by Weigl brings you media enhanced books that support active learning. Go to www.av2books.com, and enter the special code found on page 2 of this book. You will gain access to enriched and enhanced content that supplements and complements this book. Content includes video, audio, weblinks, quizzes, a slide show, and activities.

Audio
Listen to sections of the book read aloud.

Video
Watch informative video clips.

Embedded Weblinks
Gain additional information for research.

Try This!
Complete activities and hands-on experiments.

WHAT'S ONLINE?

Try This!	Embedded Weblinks	Video	EXTRA FEATURES
Identify the features of the White House. Imagine that you are designing the White House. Test your knowledge of the White House.	Learn about other rooms in the White House. Find out the details of the White House's construction. Tour the rooms of the White House.	Take a 3-D tour of the White House and its grounds. See how the White House prepares for Christmas.	**Audio** Listen to sections of the book read aloud. **Key Words** Study vocabulary, and complete a matching word activity. **Slide Show** View images and captions, and prepare a presentation. **Quizzes** Test your knowledge.

AV² was built to bridge the gap between print and digital. We encourage you to tell us what you like and what you want to see in the future.
Sign up to be an AV² Ambassador at www.av2books.com/ambassador.